The Nightingale

The Nightingale

together with
Hymns from the Office of the Passion of the Lord

Attributed to Saint Bonaventure

Freely adapted into English verse by

ROBERT NIXON

RESOURCE *Publications* • Eugene, Oregon

THE NIGHTINGALE
together with Hymns from the Office of the Passion of the Lord

Resource Publications
An Imprint of Wipf and Stock Publishers
199 W. 8th Ave., Suite 3
Eugene, OR 97401

www.wipfandstock.com

PAPERBACK ISBN: 978-1-7252-6175-4
HARDCOVER ISBN: 978-1-7252-6176-1
EBOOK ISBN: 978-1-7252-6177-8

Manufactured in the U.S.A.   01/20/20

Dedicated,
with loving devotion
and humble veneration,
to the
Blessed Virgin Mary,
Queen of Heaven,
Source of our joy,
Portal of Paradise,
Mystical rose,
Fairest of maidens,
Mother of God,
And disciple who stood most faithfully
by the cross of your divine Son.

Quod si me lyricis vatibus inseres,
sublimi feriam sidera vertice.
—Horace

Poor melancholy bird—that all night long
Tell'st to the Moon thy tale of tender woe;
From what sad cause can such sweet sorrow flow,
And whence this mournful melody of song?

Thy poet's musing fancy would translate
What mean the sounds that swell thy little breast,
When still at dewy eve thou leav'st thy nest,
Thus to the listening Night to sing thy fate?

Pale Sorrow's victims wert thou once among,
Tho' now released in woodlands wild to rove?
Say—hast thou felt from friends some cruel wrong,
Or died'st thou—martyr of disastrous love?

Ah! Songstress sad! that such my lot might be,
To sigh, and sing at liberty—like thee!

Sonnet to the Nightingale,
Charlotte Smith (1749–1806)

Contents

Translator's Note

The text variously known in Latin as *Philomela* or *Philomena* (in English 'The Nightingale') is an extended, complex and highly developed poetical composition, describing the mystical life of the soul, intertwined with both the legend of a nightingale's dying day and the story of the gospel. Traditionally—both in many manuscript sources and in the early printed editions—the work was attributed to the great Franciscan mystic and scholastic theologian, St. Bonaventure of Bagnoregio (1221–1274), popularly known as the 'Seraphic Doctor.' As well as serving as Cardinal Bishop of Albano, Bonaventure was the seventh Minister-General of the Order of Friars Minor, the great movement of spiritual renewal founded by St. Francis of Assisi. An astonishingly prolific author, his writings including many volumes of scholastic and mystical theology; and also a small quantity of poetry, of haunting beauty, lilting musicality and striking emotional intensity.

The Nightingale employs the fable of the dying day of this mysterious bird—with its fervent ascent towards the heights and inspired outbursts of ebullient song—to represent both the journey of the soul towards eternity, and the stages of the life (and particularly the passion) of Jesus Christ. According to venerable legend, when the nightingale reaches the day on which it is destined to die, with a kind of instinctive prescience it ascends the highest tree it can find. On that day, the legend relates, it will sing more beautifully and passionately than ever before.

From the top of its tree, it first heralds the dawn with a joyful outpouring of song. This song then becomes increasingly fervent and progressively more intense as the day progresses. At the third hour (nine o'clock in the morning), the singing, retaining all its agility and energy, begins to grow agitated and troubled, yet without losing anything of its enchanting sweetness. It reaches its peak at noon, when it seems that the very intensity of the singing will cause the delicate bird to burst its tiny heart and throat asunder. Indeed, from the sixth hour (noon) until the ninth hour (three o'clock in the afternoon), the bird is effectively enwrapped in the throes of death, the agonies of its final demise. Yet all the while, it continually gushes forth divine song with an ardent, celestial poetry, inflamed with an almost inebriated fervor, in which pain and bliss are mixed in dionysian abandonment.

Of course, the poignant analogy, both on a narrative and spiritual level, with the death of Christ upon the cross is inescapably clear. Following the ninth hour—the hour of death—the theme of Resurrection assumes the foreground. This is a glorious and transcendent renewal and purification, emerging, paradoxically, from the abject darkness and thanatic *kenosis* of death. Death, despite its pain and finality, is presented as both the consummation and the apotheosis of love and of life. It becomes the portal to supernal, divine peace, to ineffable joy and to eternal bliss.

This narrative scheme is reflected and embodied in both the story of the death of the nightingale and the passion of Christ. Yet it also functions as an analogical description of the soul's journey and progress in the spiritual life. The progress of the spiritual life is thus divided into 'stages'—initial joy and fervor, followed by a stage of increasing agitation and pain, and finally culminating in an event of 'death' or self- transcendence, whereby true and lasting beatitude is achieved. The attempt to divide spiritual 'progress' into such stages, following a wide variety of possible schemata, was a typical and favorite pre-occupation of authors of the time. It can be witnessed in exemplary fashion in such works as Bonaventure's own *De Triplici Via* ('The Triple Way') or his *Itinerarium Mentis in Deum* ('The Journey of the Mind into God').

One of the interesting literary features of the work is the seamless blending of the descriptions of the life and death of the nightingale, with those of the life and death of Christ—and, in turn, with the progress of the soul pursuing its spiritual path. Distinctions and stages are, it seems, deliberately rendered nebulous and blurred. All the while, the text overflows with vivid imagery, and the colorful language is richly and iridescently multivalent.

It is pertinent to note that the attribution of *The Nightingale* to Bonaventure is not without its difficulties, complexities and reservations. Indeed, several apparently reliable manuscript sources give the author as an Englishman, John Peckham (1230–1292). Peckham entered the Franciscan Order at Oxford while a relative youth, and became a disciple of Bonaventure while studying at the University of Paris. He was deeply and lastingly influenced by Bonaventure, in his love of both poverty and learning, and his embrace of a passionately christocentric and incarnational spirituality. He served as Archbishop of Canterbury from 1279 until his death, working tirelessly to improve ecclesiastical discipline and clerical integrity, and produced a modest corpus of writings—comprising mostly works of a polemic and philosophical nature. Whether or not the poem came from the pen of Peckham rather than Bonaventure himself (as the evidence does indeed credibly suggest, and many contemporary scholars opine), it is fair to describe it as being—both on a spiritual and literary level—a most wonderful expression and beautiful manifestation of the 'school of Bonaventure'.

The original Latin text is composed in rhyming trochaic verse. This simple but distinctive metrical idiom has been closely emulated in the present English rendering; with, however, some very slight and unavoidable adjustments to the rhyme scheme, insofar as they are necessitated by the differing traits of the respective languages. Nevertheless, it is hoped that the effect of the English verse substantially replicates something of the musicality, momentum and regularity of the original.

This volume also include the various hymns from the *Officium de Passione Domini* ('Office of the Passion of the Lord'), composed by Bonaventure. This collection of hymns forms a most suitable 'companion piece' to the *Nightingale*, using the various hours of the day (in this case, the canonical hours of prayer) as vantage points for meditation upon the death of Christ. In the Latin original, the language of the hymns is simple and vigorous, and the metrical scheme straightforward and clear (rhyming quatrains of the ubiquitous iambic tetrameter). This structure and quality has been reproduced as far as possible in the English renderings. However, the translator has taken the small liberty of employing trochaic tetrameter catalectic, to avoid the somewhat 'wooden' and pedestrian character which iambic meters have acquired in the English tongue (arguably the unfortunate result of six centuries of habitual over-use).

To present these masterworks of late medieval Latin mystical poetry in English verse is, for this translator, a true 'labor of love'; yet not one, it is hoped, that will be found to be entirely devoid of utility or interest for the contemporary reader.

It is perhaps here pertinent to insert a certain *apologia* or *caveat*—any attempts at 'verse translations' of poetry (including the ones included herein) necessarily partake of the character of paraphrases or adaptations, to some extent or another. A rigorously literal translation of a poetic text would seldom, if ever, reproduce the patterns of rhyme and rhythm that are constitutive of metrical poetry, and wherein much of its beauty, substance and even 'meaning' lies. For this reason, it is suggested that a 'free adaptation' (such as those here undertaken) may often more closely approach and more faithfully reproduce the effect and spirit of the original, than a punctiliously direct 'literal translation' could ever do. It is earnestly hoped that such may be found to be the case—at least for some readers—in the present small volume.

The success or otherwise of this endeavor is, of course, for others to judge. Nevertheless, the reader is humbly requested that whatever herein is deemed meritorious and edifying be attributed to the wisdom and eloquence of the original author(s) (be it Bonaventure or Peckham); but whatever is defective or inept be blamed entirely upon me,

The humble translator,
ROBERT NIXON, osb,
Abbey of the Most Holy Trinity,
New Norcia, Western Australia

Introductory Invocation

TO SAINT BONAVENTURE

Bonaventure, pensive mystic,
Oracle of sweet delight,
Never may our musings falter,
Always lead us by thy light;
Vestal flame, coruscant guide-star,
Educating yearning hearts,
Not with specious wisdom, but the
Truth which highest bliss imparts.
Urge us on, with words sublime;
Rend our hearts, our thoughts refine;
Ever sing of Love divine,

O Seraphic Doctor!

I.

Nightingale, thou songstress lovely,
Thou whose notes celestial soar,
Soothing sorrow with thy singing,
Visit me, I thee implore!

O thou pinioned sprite of music,
Who, by silvern singing, bless
Umbrous woods and silent air with
Sweetly sounding loveliness.

Let thy siren-throated warbling
With vesperic breezes blend,
Thou whose note announces gladness—
Harbinger of winter's end!

Come, o come, that I may send thee
Whither I may not yet go,
Bearing with thee hidden sweetness,
Which thy tongue alone does know!

Fly, fleet winged, to my Beloved,
Greeting him with dulcet tone;
Tell, blithe bird, of my heart's yearning,
Of my love for him alone.

And, perchance, if one should ask thee
Wherefore thou my message bring?
Be it known that thy high nature
Makes thee meet to meet my King.

II.

O my friends, hear now my verses
Telling of this hallowed bird,
Which, in mystic signs, pre-figures
Jesus, God's incarnate Word.

For this bird, when death approaches,
Bold, the highest tree ascends,
And, in giving forth its spirit,
To the skies, pure music sends.

On the last of its days mortal
When first glows the golden dawn
And, from east, the sunrise beckons,
Then its sweetest song is born.

As the light progresses duly,
Day's third hour now drawing nigh,
Then the bird, in voice unceasing,
Lets notes more exalted fly.

But when noontide heat burns brightest,
And the sun attains its peak,
Then what strains, enflamed with fervor,
Flow forth, febrile, from its beak!

Shall its throat now burst asunder?
Shall its heart with passion break?
As the ninth hour, swathed in darkness,
Comes, dear life the bird forsakes.

Gloom cimmerian grows ascendant,
Death its shadow wan does cast,
Songs hush to perpendent silence;
Beats the heart its throe the last.

Thus the cantrix sweet expires;
Thus its tiny soul repays
To the God who from dust formed it,
There to sing eternal lays.

In this gentle tale of nature,
Mystic truths are deep inscribed,
Of the Savior, holy Jesus,
Who for sinners bled and died.

And, in symbol, truths once hidden
Of the soul devout are shown,
Singing in ambrosial measures,
Flying to high realms unknown.

For these hours in signs prophetic
Show the boons God shall bestow
On the heart that fain would follow,
On the exile here below . . . .

III.

Daybreak!—lo, the time when Adam
Was from earthly slime first born;
And the hour when God incarnate
Deigned to share our state forlorn.

Aureate this lucent morning,
Skies, with hyalescence, glow.
Verbum, vere, caro factum—
Phoebus, radiant, forth does go.

Then the third hour shows the time of
Labor, which all mortals bear;
And of Christ's most holy mission,
Sowing Truth with loving care.

But at that most woeful juncture,
When the sixth hour, burning, came,
Bound he was by hands perfidious,
Whipped and scourged, and put to shame.

Spat upon by lips unholy,
Filth-like, trampled to the ground,
Offered gall, libation acrid,
And with bloody thorns was crowned.

Finally, the ninth hour fallen,
His last breath to God commends,
As the Son, divine and holy,
To plutonian depths descends,

To tartarean realms of shadow,
To the braes of gloaming grim,
Where, in opaque desolation,
Dwell the hierodules of sin.

Yet therefrom rose he victorious
And, immortal, thus did win
Triumph over Satan's thanedom—
Paid, in blood, the price of sin.

Meditating on such wonders,
Shall each soul then come to know
That it too must climb the branches
Of the tree that for it grows;

Yea, the tree of trial predestined
To each soul, that it may share
In the triumph of its Savior,
In the crown that he does wear.

IV.

Like the songbird, music raising,
So the soul greets Faith's new morn,
Hailing Truth's bold revelation,
Singing to salvation's dawn.

As the bird, proclaiming sunlight,
Does rich descants improvise,
To accompany the daystar's
Advent; so the heart shall rise

To its Maker, and shall utter:
"Praise to thee, great Lord of Love,
Thou who formed me from dark chaos,
Bidding me to bliss above!

"Oh, how great the noble honor
That on me thou first did give,
When thou made me in thine image,
Calling me in thee to live!

"For thou willed me to be sharer
In thy glorious life divine,
And thy joys—supernal, endless!—
Through thy grace, enjoy as mine.

"As a Father, thou would teach me;
As a nurse, my needs fulfil;
One with thee in joy and blessing,
One with thee in heart and will.

"What response may then I offer
But by loving totally
And adore in faith unceasing,
Weaving hymns of praise to thee?

"O my sweetest, secret nectar!
Purest gold immune to rust,
O my hope, unique and holy,
I my all to thee entrust."

Thus the soul proclaims, rejoicing,
To the Artist of all things,
In an ecstasy of praises,
To its Lord and God it sings.

So we pass through life's first dawning,
Crystal dew still glistening fresh:
So the time of Christ's appearing,
Virgin-born, in tender flesh.

V.

Then the heart, as vision sharpens,
Starts, with love, to throb and melt;
Touched it is by troublous tingling,
Heretofore unknown, unfelt.

Languishing, lamenting, plaintive,
Awestruck now, does voice resound:
"O thou, font of sweetest mercy,
Why art thou in such state found?

"Lowly, wrapped in rudest fabric,
In the garb of poverty?
What could overcome the Monarch
Of the endless sky and sea?

"Naught, indeed, but love most fervent,
Naught, but burning charity;
Naught but this could ever lower
God's own self to infancy."

Perfect infant, sweet child peerless!
Blest are they who thee embrace!
Blest is *she* who chastely kisses
Thy small hands, and feet, and face.

Would that I, with Heaven's Virgin,
Could my God in arms enfold,
And with tender care consoling,
His small limbs in my hands hold!

Would that I could dry most gently
Holy tears that his face stain;
O, to give him balm condoling,
To erase each childhood pain!

And the bliss untold, surpassing,
When should smile that infant King,
Or in tinkling strains of laughter,
Cause the air with joy to ring!

How immense the blissful blessing
Maiden Mary did enjoy,
Serving God as loving handmaid,
Chosen Mother of this Boy!

Though, O Maid, thou be the Queen of
Angels and of every star,
To be Mother of this infant
Does surpass all these by far.

Gemmed thy crown with lights celestial,
Worshipped by the seraph host;
Yet to hold thy baby, Jesus,
Does exalt thy heart the most!

Not the boundless names of honor,
But the plenitude of grace,
Gives to thee empyreal splendor,
Claims in astral heights thy place!

O, my Queen, turn thou with pity
Those thine eyes of peace divine;
Make me love thee yet more dearly,
Make my heart be ever thine!

How my soul would have exulted
Humbly to have served thy Child,
And be thralled as lowly servant
To my Virgin Queen most mild!

Thus the mind desires all hardships,
Labor then its thirst does slake;
Poverty becomes a treasure,
Hunger cherished, for love's sake,

And humility seems glorious,
Penury, a hoard of gold;
Strength is found in lowly weakness,
Trembling fear is courage bold.

VI.

But this joyous song of morning,
Soon assumes a solemn key,
As the day progresses onwards,
Till the hours, swift flown, are three.

Lo, his life is one of patience,
Hunger, thirst and want he bore;
Not amongst the rich reclining,
Walks he rather with the poor;

And on sinners, not in judgement,
But with eyes of mercy gazed;
He, consoling the afflicted,
Shared the woes of mortal days.

Tasted he this time of exile,
In this mournful vale of tears,
Sharing here our earthly sojourn,
Prey to dolor, grief and fears.

Cries his soul in notes of passion,
Tones of God's true nightingale,
Purest love its theme and burden,
Love which over sin prevails.

Song mellifluous and ardent,
Which the heart and hearing thrills!
Fervid tones of deepest yearning,
Melismatic, gemmed with trills.

O thou bird of subtle plumage,
O thou songstress, lithe of flight!
Pain transforming into pleasure,
Dancing in cerulean light.

And what secrets does thy voice tell,
What the verities it sings?
It prescribes the pathway narrow,
That the soul to Heaven brings:

Yea, the pathway of repentance—
For our God forgives, and he
Seeks not sinners' dark damnation,
Teaching Truth which makes hearts free.

As a lark ascending skyward,
So thou call the soul to flight,
Fettered not by weight of riches,
But by poverty made light;

Seeking after peace eternal,
And the glory that endures,
Not entrapped by vain deceptions,
Nor ensnared by earthly lures.

Thou did show unequalled mercy
To the penitent in tears,
Magdalene, of sin regretful—
Hers a tale of wasted years;

And of love in squalor squandered,
For the wealth that does not last;
Melancholy, fetid ashes—
For sin's feast is virtue's fast.

Happy those who heard this Teacher;
And in hearing, hungered more,
Words of heliconian splendor,
Surging to transcendent shores.

And in tasting this pure nectar,
Worldly things do vapid seem;
For, compared to Jesus' presence,
All else is but empty dream . . . .

VII.

As the mind, in meditation,
Does thus contemplate such things,
Flame celestial now ignites it,
And it strives, on love-plumed wings,

To proclaim, in strains yet higher,
God's divine, immortal praise.
So concludes the third of hours,
Of the soul's symbolic day . . .

Growing fervent now and heated,
Does the heart in passion cry;
Tears with praise now freely mingling,
For the Lamb who for it died.

In this time, as one made drunken,
With intoxicating wine,
It, inebriated, flounders,
Senses lost in love divine.

As the noontide, hot and fulvid,
Now its apex does attain,
Vein and heart with love are punctured,
Sharing in the cross's pain.

Seeing now the Lamb beloved—
Stainless Lamb that for it bled—
Crowned with thorns, tormented, hated,
Mocked with purple, cruelly led

To that Hill of Skulls, blood-blackened,
Where, with nails, his flesh was torn.
Smeared with blood that face angelic,
Pallid, downcast and forlorn.

"Sad I am," the soul's plaint bitter,
"Sad my eyes, that they behold
Jesus Christ, my heart's beloved,
Languishing in pain untold.

"Why dost thou, my love, thus suffer?
Why dost thou, my love, thus die?
Is it for my sins' atonement
That thou on this cross must lie?"

Bitter pain is this salvation,
Sweet, though, is its bitterness;
Death is love's true consummation,
Death is love's most holy kiss.

Thou, O Christ, are springtide newness,
Thou, the wine of fresh desire;
Honeyed flavor, all-surpassing
Bloom exquisite, born of fire!

Let the penitent believe that
Christ's death serves the soul to save;
So will Satan's schemes be thwarted,
Though in vain Hell's fiends may rave.

What great love ensnared thee, Jesus,
Drew thee to this pit of pain?
Can it be that thou sought only
Souls once lost for God to gain?

As a fish, on sharp hook captured,
So were thou by love beset,
Pierced by nails with lost souls baited,
Trapped in mercy's holy net.

Little wonder, then, if I shall
Sigh for thee, with fervent breath,
Thou who for my soul so wretched
Did embrace that tree of death!

Let me heart with thine now suffer,
Let me in thy wounds be hid,
Perfectly with thee united,
Living, dying as thou did!

VIII.

Burn within me flames of longing,
Dark-hued love which scalds my soul,
Love which is the sweetest torment,
Yearnings deep, beyond control . . . .

Lo, the spear I see approaching,
Instrument of cruellest harm,
Raised to pierce thy flesh of iv'ry:
Forth thence flows that precious balm,

Balm of blood divine, and water,
Flowing as a crimson tide,
Running forth, as healing nectar,
From the font of Jesus' side.

Rubicund, yet clear as crystal,
Brook pellucid with love's light;
To the sorrowful, nepenthe;
To a blind world, purer sight.

Richer than the gold of orient,
Rarer than the ocean's pearl,
Drops of love, distilled salvation,
Running down, a blood-stained swirl,

Soaking earth with deep forgiveness,
Making hardened hearts to yield,
Drenching deserts with its moisture,
Leaving viridescent fields.

Key of Paradise resplendent,
Wound which all our wounds does heal,
Love which all the realms has conquered,
Which each heart makes love to feel!

Holy, glorious, gentle river,
Stream of sacramental life,
Waters of the new creation,
Cleansing sin, and calming strife.

Like the lark of night-song dying
In the fire of noontide sun,
Cries the soul in pain ecstatic,
While its strains, delirious, run.

One it is with its Beloved,
One with death, and one with love,
Heart now bursting in its frenzy,
Panting for the realms above,

Till the climax be accomplished.
God's own voice, in tones sublime,
'*CONSUMMATUM EST*,' now thunders,
Loquent silence halting time.

IX.

Darkened stands the earthly kingdom,
Sable stand the depths of space:
As the ninth hour, grim and fateful,
Takes its due and ordered place.

Weeps the welkin, tears forth flowing,
At the death of God's true Son.
From the rocks, by sorrow ruptured,
Rills of saline blackness run.

But as deepest, ebon darkness
Heralds nigh approach of dawn,
So this death announces triumph.
As a Phoenix, fire-born,

Rises from the ashen debris
Unto light and life anew,
So the cross has opened Heaven,
Flooded earth with lambent dew.

Unsealed are the gates celestial,
Lifted is the ancient curse,
As the cross the fatal sentence
On Eve's children does reverse.

Adam's progeny, once sunk in
Lachrymose amaritude,
Skyward soar on noble pinions,
Pristine innocence renewed.

Let us sing no lamentation,
Neither threnody, nor dirge—
Jesus, our eternal Savior,
From this mortal pyre shall surge,

Clad in glory more than human,
Robed in majesty divine,
Rising as the vernal orchid,
Or fresh blossom of the vine,

As the rose of deathless glory,
As the amaranthine flower,
Radiating grace resplendent,
Beauty's all-embracing power.

So the soul, embraced in rapture,
Feels the kisses, chaste and pure,
Of its Spouse, its one Beloved,
Who shall hold it evermore.

Tears have ceased, the waters bitter
No more sting the mournful eye;
Rather joy beyond all measure
Strives with spirit-wings to fly!

Nothing more is there to hope for,
Endless joy forever gained;
No more tears, nor death, nor sorrow;
No regret, nor sin, nor pain.

And the heart sings 'Hallelujah!',
Tasting, sweet, its Lover's kiss,
Lost in God's eternal splendor,
Now dissolved in nameless bliss . . . .

X.

Let me finish here these stanzas,
Lest that I may tedious prove.
Sighs, not words, befit the seeker;
Love, not verses, spirits move.

If, O gentle, kindly reader,
In my humble song, thou find
Ought but empty, broken phrases,
Ought that moves thy heart or mind,

Give, then, to thy God the glory,
Strum to him on lute of praise,
Imitate the nightingale,
Sing to him throughout thy days.

Strike, with love, thy harp of longing,
Sound to God thy hidden chord,
Thy Beloved serenading,
Lauding ceaselessly thy Lord.

Learn the hymn that saints and seraphs,
Martyrs, virgins, angels too,
Sing in joyful adoration
To their God, unseen yet true.

Let this sound within thy soul's depths
In unfettered unison,
To the Father and the Spirit,
And the glorious, risen Son!

Doing thus be thou united
To the high olympian choirs,
In the wedding everlasting,
With the Love thy heart desires . . . .

Amen.
Deo gratias.

Hymns from the
Office of the Passion of the Lord

by St. Bonaventure

adapted by Robert Nixon, osb

HYMN FOR MATINS

In the Lord's most holy cross,
Which restored sweet Eden's loss,
Bides a refuge ever sure,
Truest hope of hearts made pure!

Let us ever mindful be
Of Christ's doleful agony,
Of the crown of thorns he wore—
Torments which for us he bore,

And the wounds in limbs and side,
Pouring forth love's crimson tide;
Whips, and gall and bitter wine
Proffered to those lips divine!

In such things, let hearts be sunk—
Lost, inebriated, drunk!
Let the cross's branch take root
In our souls, and bear rich fruit.

Let us honor fervently
That redeeming gallows tree,
And, amongst the saints, Christ's praise
Peal with joy for endless days!

Praise and glory to God's Son,
Scorned and sold, betrayed and shunned:
Thus died Christ to save the lost,
Paid in blood sin's dreadful cost!

HYMN FOR LAUDS

Monarch, who unrivalled reign—
Bane of sin's promethic chain—
We to thee all laud now raise;
Seraph hosts enjoin thy praise!

Lo, the bitter pangs thou felt
Makes each human heart to melt,
Makes them burn with love for thee,
Aching, yearning fervently.

O, each scourge and bitter blow
Does unfathomed mercy show!
Through these is the grace of Heav'n
To the earth-bound exile giv'n.

Let thy blood tint every heart;
To each eye, pure tears impart.
Through thy laving, souls are cleaned;
Through thy wounds is life redeemed!

Through thy passion's potent kiss,
Fill us, Lord, with secret bliss!
For supernal joys thou give
To all souls who in thee live.

Praise and glory to the Son,
Scorned and sold, betrayed and shunned:
Thus died Christ to save the lost,
Paid in blood sin's fearful cost!

PRAYER

Lord Jesus Christ—who at the dawning hour of sunrise willed to give thyself up for the salvation of the human race, to be struck, bound, whipped and spat upon—make us, we entreat thee, gladly and courageously to accept all the humiliations and opprobrium of this life for the sake of the glory of God's most holy name, and continually to be mindful of thy glorious and sacred passion, so that we may merit to be sharers in the unending felicity of a glorious Resurrection!

HYMN FOR PRIME

Thou, the sun of justice bright,
Clouded by sin's sable night,
Mocked in royal purple robes,
Striped by scourges, bruised by blows.

Seized were thou by brutal hands,
Made before thy judge to stand,
Yet you uttered not a word,
Yea, no plaint from thee was heard.

O, we beg thee earnestly
To receive us clemently,
And, for gentle mercy's sake,
Open Heaven's azure gate!

Praise and glory to the Son,
Scorned and sold, betrayed and shunned:
Thus died Christ to save the lost,
Paid in blood sin's ghastly cost!

PRAYER

Lord Jesus Christ, supreme judge of the Universe, divine potentate of unrivalled puissance—who at the first hour of the day, for the sake of us sinners, meekly and silently stood before Pilate to accept this world's most cruel judgement—to thee we humbly pray that thou mercifully assist us, in our own personal hour of judgement, to escape the dire and adamantine sentence of eternal damnation and unending death; but rather that we may merit to be joined forever with the celestial ranks of the faithful in thy glorious presence.

HYMN FOR TERCE

In this third hour of the day,
Thou, O Lord, were led away
To the knoll of Calvary,
There to mount that baleful tree!

Bruised and pierced and cruelly nailed;
Nary, though, thy patience failed.
Lo, the cross becomes thy throne,
Testament of grace unknown.

Make us love thee more and more—
Thee, sweet Jesus, to adore—
That one day we may find rest
In thy realms of glory blest!

Praise and glory to the Son,
Scorned and sold, betrayed and shunned:
Thus died Christ to save the lost,
Paid in blood sin's gruesome cost!

PRAYER

Lord Jesus Christ, Son of the living God—who at the third hour of the day were led to the tortures and torments of the cross, for the salvation of the world—we pray to thee with earnest supplication that, by virtue of thy most holy passion, thou cleanse us from every stain of sin and from all pollution of prevarication, leading propitiously to the everlasting glory of Heaven's supreme beatitude!

HYMN FOR SEXT

By the cross's weight oppressed,
And by acrid thirst distressed,
Jesus, whom did scorners fierce
Beat and mock, deride and pierce!

Tortures nameless did he carry;
To endure, though, scorned to tarry,
This—behold!—is love's true price,
Passion's highest sacrifice.

Honor, yea, is due to him—
Lord of Love, and star-throned King—
He who through his bitter pain
Life immortal did obtain.

Praise and glory to the Son,
Scorned and sold, betrayed and shunned:
Thus died Christ to save the lost,
Paid in tears our sorrow's cost.

PRAYER

Lord Jesus Christ—who at the sixth hour ascended the fearful gibbet of the cross, upon which, thirsting for our salvation, the most bitter and tetric goblet of gall and vinegar was offered to thy gentle lips—we beseech thee to imbue us with a burning thirst for the golden chalice of thy passion, our hearts ever ablaze with ardent love for thee!

HYMN FOR NONE

May death's holy consummation,
Bring salvific liberation:
May our Savior's agony,
Win for us eternity.

In his death is life divine;
His embrace—enchanting wine!
Though his fleshly lamp expire,
Glows undimmed love's fulgid fire.

Jesus, in his dying breath,
Triumphed, victor over death.
He this woeful world did save,
By descent into the grave!

Praise and glory to the Son,
Scorned and sold, disdained and shunned:
Thus died Christ to save the lost,
Paid in pain love's noble cost!

PRAYER

*Lord Jesus Christ—who at the grim and fearful ninth hour, with hands
extended in ineffable love and with head bowed down in supreme humility,
did surrender thy spirit to God the Father of light; and, by the key of thy
most holy death, unlocked the sidereal portals of the celestial Elysium—
grant that, at the hour of our own death, our souls may fly unto thee, who
are thyself the truest Paradise and the highest Heaven!*

HYMN FOR VESPERS

Lord, thou broke the chains that bound us,
Shattered darksome walls around us;
Lead us to eternal peace,
From our woes, grant us release.

Thou once drained that bitter cup,
On the bread of tears did sup;
For our sins, thou deigned to die,
King eternal, Lord most high!

Grant salvation to the world;
Let love's banner be unfurled!
Save us from our sin and pain;
Free us from these mortal chains.

From the cross's torrid altar
Flowed forth freely blood and water;
Blood most noble, crystalline
Water, from thy flesh divine.

Sacrosanct and precious blood,
Bear us, in thy ruby flood,
To the wedding feast above,
To the banquet of pure love.

Praise and glory to the Son,
Who unending life has won:
Thus died Christ to save the lost,
Paid in blood love's holy cost!

PRAYER

Lord Jesus Christ—who at the twilight hour of eventide were lowered, lifeless, from the dark tree of the cross, and whose tender, broken body was thence placed in the loving hands of thy most dolorous Mother—mercifully grant that we, freed from the heavy burden of our sins, may one day stand, rejoicing in the unfettered liberty of true innocence, in the sight of thy divine majesty!

HYMN FOR COMPLINE

Jesus, who for love did die,
In the earth, entombed, to lie;
Teach our hearts to rest with thee,
In thy silence, rendered free.

Charon's stream thou, bold, did sail,
Entered Sheol's lightless vale.
In thy slumber, grant us peace;
In thy sleep, despair's surcease.

Help us, Lord, who gave thyself
That we be restored to health;
Lead us through the battle's strife,
To thine own eternal life.

Endless glory to the Son,
With the Godhead ever one,
Christ who died to save the lost,
Gave his heart, love's highest cost . . . .

PRAYER

Lord Jesus Christ—who at the final hour of the day rested in the tenebrous recesses of a stony sepulchre, mourned and bewailed with the fervent and inconsolable lamentations of thy most blessed Mother and other faithful and holy women—make us, we pray, always to abound with tears of sincere and indefatigable compunction, and unceasingly to lament in our hearts thy holy passion—both supremely bitter and ineffably glorious—

with a love most ardent, and a devotion ever true;

Who live and reign with the Father and the Holy Spirit—

Trinity of perfect love—

one God forever and ever.

Amen.